Non*monogamy* **&**
Betrayal

Also by Eve Rickert

The New More Than Two
A Philosophical Reimagining
by Eve Rickert and Andrea Zanin
Thornapple Press, 2026

Originally published in hardcover in 2024
as More Than Two, Second Edition.

More Than Two Essentials

Non_monogamy_ & **Betrayal**

Eve Rickert

Thornapple Press, 300-722 Cormorant Street
Victoria, BC V8W 1P8 Canada press@thornapplepress.ca

EU Authorised Representative: Easy Access System Europe – Mustamäe tee 50, 10621 Tallinn, Estonia, gpsr.requests@easproject.com

Our business offices are located on the traditional, ancestral and unceded territories of the lək̓ʷəŋən and W̱SÁNEĆ peoples. We return a percentage of company profits to the original stewards of this land through South Island Reciprocity Trust.

Thornapple Press is a brand of Talk Science to Me Communications Inc. Talk Science is a WBE Canada Certified Women Business Enterprise, a CGLCC Certified 2SLGBTQI+-owned business, and a Certified Living Wage Employer.

Design by Jeff Werner and Cassie Clay-Smith
Substantive editing by Andrea Zanin, Alana Phelan and Erin Wiegand
Copy-editing and proofreading by Heather van der Hoop and Alison Whyte

Library and Archives Canada Cataloguing in Publication

Title: Nonmonogamy and betrayal / Eve Rickert.
Names: Rickert, Eve, author
Description: Series statement: More than two essentials ; 12 | Includes bibliographical references.
Identifiers: Canadiana (print) 20250330334 | Canadiana (ebook) 20250330369 | ISBN 9781990869792
(softcover) | ISBN 9781990869808 (EPUB) | ISBN 9781990869938 (PDF)
Subjects: LCSH: Non-monogamous relationships. | LCSH: Non-monogamous relationships—Psychological aspects. | LCSH: Betrayal. | LCSH: Trust.
Classification: LCC HQ980 .R54 2025 | DDC 306.84/23—dc23

Printed and bound in the United States of America by Publishers Graphics.
10 9 8 7 6 5 4 3 2 1

To everyone who helped inspire this book.

"Of course I'll hurt you. Of course you'll hurt me. Of course we will hurt each other. But this is the very condition of existence. To become spring, means accepting the risk of winter."

— Antoine de Saint-Exupéry,
The Little Prince

Contents

Acknowledgements

The first draft of this book was dictated into my cell phone from the lower bunk of a riverside cabin in an Ecuadorian cloud forest. Alana Phelan stitched these transcripts together into something I could loosely call a manuscript, and Andrea Zanin's patient guidance helped me shape it into something I could confidently call a book. Erin Wiegand provided further substantive refinements. I am grateful to the whole team at Thornapple—Heather, Jeff, Cassie, Alison and Emily—who pulled out the stops to get this book out on a short timeline. And especially to Hazel, for putting up with my many delays and not letting me give up on the book. And as always, to Shelly, for the conversations and insight.

Introduction

Nonmonogamy has shaped the landscape of my adult life for decades—publicly, intellectually and in the quiet interior places where relationships leave their marks.

It's more than a relationship structure for me; it's a political and ethical project. I've spent years writing, editing and publishing work intended to guide nonmonogamous folks toward more integrity, more care and less hyperbole about freedom without responsibility. I've also spent years living inside the contradictions of this practice—where our ideals collide with our blind spots, where harm goes unnamed because we don't yet agree on foundational ethical principles. This book grows out of that fault line.

In my own nonmonogamous relationships, I have found myself navigating experiences that feel in my nervous system like betrayal but that I have been unable to easily identify as such—and so, have had difficulty addressing, personally or interpersonally. I have had conflicts in my relationships that felt perpetually unresolved, because the core of the pain for me, an experience of injustice, went unrecognized, unwitnessed and unaccounted for. This feeling of erasure has come from partners, from friends and community members, and from within. And I know I am not the only one who has these experiences. The idea and outline for this book dropped into my head after a particularly profound betrayal by a former romantic partner, but it took me another two years to turn it into this short little book. Betrayal is hard to talk about and even harder to understand.

> Betrayal changes your relationship with yourself, with other people and with the rest of the world, sometimes permanently.

But why write a book about betrayal specifically, when there are so many ways that nonmonogamy can hurt? In nonmonogamy discussion groups, podcasts and books, it's common to hear about topics like jealousy, time management and power differentials, but in my experience, it's rare to hear the word betrayal. I think it's hard to receive validation or care for experiences of betrayal in nonmonogamy in the same way that we might for some of these other kinds of struggles. This is a shame, because betrayal leaves a particular kind of damage. It does more than hurt: Betrayal changes your relationship with yourself, with other people and with the rest of the world, sometimes permanently.

I think many kinds of betrayals are specific to nonmonogamy, because we've largely thrown away the old rule book for relationships. In monogamy, a certain set of actions and experiences are generally recognized as betrayals, and when those things happen, you get social support for them. You get recognition and resources to help deal with them. There's an entire industry of therapists, coaches, books and social media channels devoted to helping people heal from their partners' affairs, for example. We don't have much like that for betrayal in nonmonogamy—though there are plenty of "coaches" ready to help us deal with jealousy or unlearn couple privilege. We don't yet have a cultural consensus on what betrayal in nonmonogamy is.

Monogamy's well-understood rule book helps identify who is the wronged party and who is the wrongdoer, and thus who needs to make amends (or even whether amends need to be made). Cheating, after all, is cheating. The first time I experienced something in a nonmonogamous relationship that felt like "cheating," all I could find were resources for dealing with monogamous affairs. These resources acknowledge that affairs are traumatic for the cheated-upon partner, severely damage trust in long-lasting ways, and frequently lead to the end of a monogamous relationship. But I could not point to a specific agreement that had been broken, and so, by the conventional wisdom of the time (at least in my circles), my pain was my problem. To make matters worse, my partner and I did not have a clear road map for rebuilding trust that wasn't rooted in mononormativity.[1]

So if you're nonmonogamous, what even is cheating? And how do you deal with it when it happens? And what about all the other kinds of damaging, unexpected betrayals that come up in a nonmonogamous context?

This book is a meditation on what betrayal is, the specific and nuanced ways it shows up in nonmonogamous relationships, and how we can begin to repair our relationships—and ourselves—after it happens. It's not my intention to try to give you a definitive answer to how to "fix" betrayal in nonmonogamy or hand you a rule book you can use to prove who the villain in your relationship is. I want to reflect on what the experience of betrayal in nonmonogamous relationships feels like, what can cause it, the damage it can do and some ways you might begin to deal with it.

Before we dig in, I need to give a disclaimer: Unless I say so explicitly, I am talking about situations that are not abusive. While many people engage in some toxic behaviours now and then, at least until they learn better skills, genuine coercive control muddies the waters when it comes to trying to define, understand or heal from betrayal much more than I can get into here. Sometimes betrayal is part of abuse, and sometimes abuse involves bad-faith accusations of betrayal in order to make someone easier to control (misogynistic abuse notoriously includes extreme jealousy, for example). See chapter three of my last book, *The New More Than Two*[2], for a deep dive on abuse in nonmonogamy and a hefty resource list. If you think you might be in an abusive relationship, please proceed with caution as you read this book, and seek out other resources to support you as well.

I want to make these things easier to talk about. I want to legitimize the experience of betrayal in nonmonogamy as a real thing and offer tools for recognizing and witnessing it. I want to help us make true apologies and accept accountability with grace.
To do all of that, we first need to understand what betrayal really means.

What Is Trust?

Before we talk about what we mean by betrayal, we have to first talk about trust. Trust is one of those words we think we understand until we try to define it. It's easy to use casually—"I trust you," "I don't trust them," "we're rebuilding trust"—as if it's a single, self-evident thing. In fact, it's a bundle of experiences we collapse into one word.

I grew up a Quaker, and the values I learned in that community have deeply shaped my ethics as an adult. Something that is central to early Quaker practice is a preference for *faith over belief*.[3]

Belief is something concrete: a position you hold about the way things are. Maybe it was passed down to you; maybe you came to it after learning and reflection. It can be substantiated or not. But it's something you can write down. Faith, on the other hand, is alive—experiential. Belief is knowing *about* something; faith is *knowing* it.

In relationships, I think that trust is closer to faith than to belief. Trust is the state your nervous system rests in when you expect that another person will treat you with care, honesty and respect, even when the situation is ambiguous or emotionally charged. Maybe you don't know exactly what the other person will do, but trust means you feel safe in the unknowing.[4]

Trust doesn't mean you think someone will always act perfectly, or even in the way you want them to. It's an internalized expectation that they will take your well-being into account when they make choices that affect you. It's also the expectation that, when they mess up, as all of us do, they'll acknowledge the impact and try to repair. When trust is at its highest, you know that you matter, intrinsically, to someone else's decision-making, so you don't need to insert yourself into it (unless invited).

In monogamous culture, trust often gets collapsed into sexual exclusivity or the relationship escalator.[5] Nonmonogamy makes us widen the frame. If relationships are allowed to be multiple and fluid, then trust can't rest on a single behavioural prohibition, or even a complicated set of rules. It has to rest on something deeper: shared values, transparency, mutual consideration and the confidence that your partners won't use ambiguity, loopholes or manipulation to avoid accountability.

Trust is important because it shapes your relational world. When you trust someone, your body settles. It's easier to be open. You can take risks, not because you're insulated from harm, but because you feel grounded enough in the relationship to step into uncertainty. This is the "security paradox."[6] You can relax and stop constantly scanning for danger, as so many of us are doing all the time. When trust is breached, it doesn't just hurt your feelings. It changes your internal map of what (and who) is safe. It reshapes what feels possible in the relationship, and sometimes in your wider life.

Trust in a relationship or polycule requires more than integrity and consideration, though: It requires alignment. Do you have a shared, mutually understood picture of what you're doing together and what responsibilities you each feel toward the connection? Or does each of you have your own fantasy of what the relationship is or could be, one that maybe you're hoping for, expecting (without saying it) or surreptitiously trying to steer the relationship toward? When another person, an actual real, living human being, doesn't live out your narrative, the disappointment can *feel* like betrayal. But what's being ruptured isn't trust; it's a story that only one of you was writing. More on this later.

What Is Betrayal?

The simple definition of betrayal is that it's when somebody deeply violates your trust. It happens in intimate relationships, but it can also occur within polycules or community and among metamours or friends.[7]

I needed to provide a functional definition of trust before I could talk about betrayal, because betrayal isn't just "a bad thing someone did." It's the rupture of the expectation of safety. It's the moment when the world you thought you were inhabiting with someone suddenly shifts under your feet. You trusted someone, you gave them the power to hurt you, and now they have, in a way that was unexpected. I think many of us imagine that betrayal always comes from cruelty, ill will or a lack of care. But as uncomfortable as it is to acknowledge, betrayal isn't always intentional. I believe it can happen even when everyone involved is genuinely doing their best, acting with good intentions and trying to be kind. But sometimes people have such different understandings of their relationships—or such different thresholds for what feels safe—that one person's "honest mistake" or "I didn't think it would be that big a deal" lands for another as a profound violation. Intent matters, of course, and it matters a lot when you're deciding what to do next. But impact matters too, especially when part of the impact was that you didn't have the information you needed to make an informed choice. You can be hurt even if no one meant to hurt you. Because of that, in this book, I focus on the experience of betrayal, because I think it's the experience that has gone unacknowledged for so long, and it's a lot easier to define an experience than to define intent.

Betrayal hurts, but not everything that hurts is betrayal. A hurt is only a betrayal when there is a breach of trust. Lying is usually a betrayal, but only when it breaks trust. Lying to get a partner to a surprise party, or to get the upper hand in a game of Diplomacy, might not be a betrayal (but it might be, depending on your relationship!). Likewise, many betrayals involve lying—but not all of them. I'll get to some of those later.

Betrayal isn't just trust-breaking; it's trust-breaking with stakes. Not every broken expectation is a betrayal, and not every lie carries the same weight. It's a spectrum, and there's no easy dividing line between disappointment, hurt and betrayal. Whether or not broken trust becomes betrayal depends on three things: the depth of the initial trust, the meaning of the act itself and the degree to which your ability to make informed choices was taken away. A partner exaggerating their job title or pretending they were into K-Pop because they knew you were might be annoying, but it's unlikely to upend your internal sense of safety or rewrite your understanding of the relationship. Betrayal does. It strikes at the core of how you understood the relationship and your place in it. While there's no universal checklist of what "counts," betrayal has gravity: It changes something fundamental in you, the relationship, or both.

> Betrayal isn't just trust-breaking; it's trust-breaking with stakes.

Here are a few of the elements I think characterize betrayal.

BETRAYAL REMOVES AGENCY. I believe a fundamental element of betrayal is a removal of agency—your ability to consent meaningfully to the reality you are actually living—and this removal of agency is ultimately what makes betrayal so damaging. Andrea Zanin and I wrote at length about agency (and honesty!) in *The New*

More Than Two, but to summarize: Agency is your ability to make freely informed choices about things that affect you. Betrayal creates a sense of "I thought this was one thing, and it's something else. I thought I was safe, but I wasn't." And often, the person presenting the danger is someone you trusted to provide safety.

BETRAYAL REVERBERATES BACKWARD, INTO YOUR MEMORIES. One of the most awful things about severe betrayal in relationships is that it can rewrite the past. When you experience a profound betrayal, it can make you reconsider all of your past experiences with the person who betrayed you, and that whole relationship might become tainted by your new knowledge. Before the betrayal, everything you did in the relationship happened within a container of trust, probably trust that had deepened through time. After the betrayal, you might look back at all those moments of intimacy, vulnerability and joy, all the adventures, and all the wonderful times you had together, and feel that they've been reshaped by what happened (or what you learned) after them. You may even mentally and emotionally revise the entire relationship, potentially destroying any beautiful memories you may have had.

BETRAYAL CAN CHANGE THE WAY YOU SEE THE PERSON WHO BETRAYED YOU, even if you choose to stay with them. You may never trust them in the way you trusted them before. It may take a great deal of time and effort to rebuild trust, and the relationship might never be quite the same. If the other person can't accept that you experienced a betrayal, it may be difficult for them to do the kind of repair that you need in order to rebuild trust in the relationship. This can lead either to the end of the relationship or to a relationship in which the two of you never really trust each other again—which will create all kinds of other problems down the road.

BETRAYAL CAN CHANGE YOUR RELATIONSHIP WITH YOURSELF. The most profound betrayals change not only our relationship with the person who betrayed us, but our relationship with ourselves and our relationship with the rest of the world—and potentially every person we meet or try to be close to after the betrayal. When you have trusted someone deeply and they have broken that trust, it can be hard to just say, "that's a them problem." It can make you question your own judgment and discretion, imagining it was somehow your fault—that there were signs you should have seen or ways you brought it on yourself. You may end up questioning yourself, even challenging your core beliefs: "Did I trust the wrong person? Was I foolish? Was I too trusting? Am I gullible? Can I ever trust anyone again?"

BETRAYAL CAN SOW SEEDS OF DOUBT IN YOUR FUTURE RELATIONSHIPS. You may take much longer to build trust with new people (which may or may not be a good thing), and once your trust has been broken, even in small ways, it can be much harder for the person who broke it to earn it back.

If you were someone who believed that most people have some fundamental goodness in them or are doing the best they can with the tools they have, or if you were someone who tended toward optimism, then betrayal—especially repeated betrayal, and especially by more than one person—can invert this view of the world. You could find yourself becoming bitter or suspicious, always looking for ulterior motives, always waiting for the next shoe to drop.

Betrayal in Nonmonogamy

As I mentioned earlier, monogamy offers a pretty clear set of rules, which allows for a clearer definition of betrayal in monogamous contexts. Those rules have become a bit muddied with things like situationships (discussed later), microcheating and emotional affairs, but basically, everyone knows what an affair is, and everyone knows you don't do it. You just don't fall in love or have sex with with someone other than your monogamous partner. But in nonmonogamy, and more specifically polyamory, that's exactly what many people do.

We've thrown out the rule book. We customize our commitments, rewrite the rules, design our relationships, and step off the relationship escalator.[8] Every relationship is unique, we like to say—and so betrayals, when they happen, can seem to come out of left field. In a context where almost anything could be OK or not OK depending on the relationship, it's sometimes difficult to know where a boundary even is until it's been crossed.

This fluidity can be great. It allows creativity, autonomy and relationships that fit who we are rather than who others tell us to be. But it also means that the places where trust might break are as infinitely varied as the forms our relationships can take.

And it means that you can end up having your perceptions undermined if the person who betrayed you, or other people around you, do not recognize the betrayal that you experienced. They may try to convince you that you should be OK with it, that it wasn't that bad, that it was just a mistake, that you should continue to trust the other person, or that the problem is you. I think this scenario is unfortunately quite common in nonmonogamy. Especially when done by a group, it can easily become gaslighting. Too many folks will weaponize the flexibility of nonmonogamy to avoid accountability in a relationship or to avoid making waves in a polycule or community. For example: If we didn't have an agreement about it, then it can't be a betrayal. If you feel hurt, it must be mononormativity. If you need clarity, you must be hierarchical or controlling. These frameworks can silence legitimate pain and make it harder for you to name what happened.

There's also a particular kind of betrayal that emerges when someone uses the language of nonmonogamy—freedom, autonomy, relationship design—as a shield for choices that actually undermine consent. Someone can technically follow "the rules" while violating the spirit of the relationship: hiding emotional entanglements behind selective transparency, stalling difficult conversations to avoid consequences, or using ambiguity to create plausible deniability. In these cases, the betrayal isn't about sex or dating; it's about evasion, misdirection or the quiet accumulation of double meanings.

You can also experience betrayal by a group, such as when a partner teams up with a metamour or even your whole polycule. It can also come from your nonmonogamous community, if you have one. Of course, group betrayal certainly happens in monogamous relationships, and in settings outside of intimate relationships—such as when families collude to cover up cheating, addiction or abuse. But I think that the kind of trust that it's common for people to invest in their intimate nonmonogamous networks creates a unique kind of vulnerability to betrayal, and a unique kind of damage when it happens.

> Nonmonogamy's promise is that we don't have to get everything from one person; its risk is that our webs of trust multiply the number of places we can be wounded.

Polycules are social systems. We rely on them for emotional support, chosen family, belonging, and material and emotional care.

When that network turns against us, or closes ranks to protect some at the expense of others, the injury isn't just personal. It's systemic. You're not just losing a partner; you're losing a support structure, and sometimes an entire social world.

Group betrayal often compounds. If your partner hurts you and your metamour dismisses it, the hurt deepens. If your community minimizes it, it calcifies. If people close to you quietly adjust their loyalties to avoid "drama," you may feel as though the floor of your entire relational world has dropped out from under you. Nonmonogamy's promise is that we don't have to get everything from one person; its risk is that our webs of trust multiply the number of places we can be wounded.

Varieties of Betrayal in Nonmonogamy

As I've mentioned, nonmonogamy creates as many ways to break trust as it does to build it. Some betrayals happen within the relationship, inside an agreed-upon container where everyone believes they understand what they're doing together. Others are betrayals of the relationship itself, where the relationship you thought you were in wasn't quite the relationship the other person believed they were offering. Both kinds of rupture can be devastating, but they aren't the same kind of devastation. A betrayal within the relationship violates trust, but a betrayal about the relationship (also) violates reality. These distinctions matter, because the kind of betrayal you're facing shapes what recovery looks like, what is repairable, and what might not be.

I'm going to move through a range of examples, from the subtle to the severe, to offer a kind of taxonomy of the ways we trust each other in nonmonogamous relationships—and thus, the ways our trust can be broken. Perhaps counterintuitively, I am not going to discuss broken agreements. I think these are the most straightforward kinds of betrayals, the easiest ones to recognize, and for most part they aren't prone to this kind of erasure. They're also covered well in other books.[9] Instead, I want to focus on a much broader range of betrayals that I think are quite common, but aren't as easily recognized.

As I get into specific situations of betrayal, keep in mind that those arising from mistakes, misunderstandings or unintentional carelessness are very different from those arising from deceit, secrecy, manipulation or selfishness. Unless I say so directly, I'm not suggesting that someone in these situations has (necessarily) done wrong or that some kind of rule has been broken. I am not trying to moralize, point fingers or assign blame. I am trying to outline specific situations that can create an experience of betrayal—and that experience needs to be attended to whether or not anyone is actually "in the wrong."

In general, I think we can assume good intent in many of these situations, but the betrayal still needs to be witnessed and recognized, and its emotional impact deserves care within the relationship. And unfortunately, betrayal can still have long-lasting effects on the relationship, even if no one is at fault. You and the others involved will likely need to work to rebuild trust—which I'll talk about more later in this book. And if it turns out that there was ill intent, I very much hope you will decide not to continue in that relationship.

Betrayals Within the Relationship

In these betrayals, you know what you are to each other, but something still went wrong.

Let's start small, with tiny misattunements that can feel big. These may almost seem like they shouldn't carry a label as big as "betrayal"—but they add up, and sometimes the emotional experience of even one can be surprisingly outsized.

MICROBETRAYALS. Let's start with what John Gottman[10] refers to as "sliding door moments," when an intimate turns away from you at key points. They don't respond to a bid for connection, don't repair a conflict (large or small), or don't rebuild trust after a rupture. These kinds of small breaches of trust, if unaddressed, can accumulate over time to destroy a relationship. Gottman wrote about them in the context of monogamy. But in nonmonogamy, these small betrayals can be much more damaging if a partner turns away from you (or just doesn't notice your bid) and instead turns toward another partner. The availability of your metamour makes it easier for your partner to turn away from you—and so much more painful when they do. Processing with another partner after a conflict with you, or even just turning to another partner for comfort, can also become a way to avoid coming back to your relationship to repair after that conflict.

> Even small experiences of broken trust need repair.

Another common nonmonogamous experience that falls into this category comes up when you think you have a special kind of ritual or shared experience with a partner—something as simple as a song, a meal, a little routine or your favourite mushroom-foraging patch. If they do that thing with another partner without first discussing it with you, it may reveal expectations you didn't know you had. These incidents can be especially tricky to deal with because you may experience a feeling of betrayal even if your partner is not being malicious and is trying to live up to the terms of your relationship agreements. The shock isn't always about the act, but about suddenly learning that its meaning was not mutual.

Ruptures like these are rarely intentional, but they deserve witnessing. Even small experiences of broken trust need repair, or they become the sediment that later betrayals settle into.

JUSTICE JEALOUSY. Coined by Jessica Fern and David Cooley,[11] the term "justice jealousy" refers to an experience in which you have an unmet need in your relationship that has caused you pain, and you have come to believe that the thing you need is unavailable to you from your partner—but then they turn around and give that thing to another partner. In *Polywise*, Jessica describes how early in their relationship, David would not engage in planning dates with her, to the point where she had come to accept that it just wasn't part of who he was—until the day she got a verification text asking her to approve David's login to their Airbnb account so that he could plan a getaway with a new partner.

It could be something that seems trivial from the outside. Perhaps you have been trying to get a partner to go out dancing with you for years, and they've shown absolutely no interest. Then they find a new partner who loves dancing, and suddenly they're going out every Friday night. Or perhaps you've been asking for months for a partner to set an expectation of how often they can see you, but they insist that they just aren't the kind of person who can offer that kind of reliability. Just as you've come to accept that loving them as they are means accepting that you won't ever get an established routine, they come back from the third date with a new partner and casually drop that the two of them just agreed to see each other once a week. Suddenly that kind of commitment is no big deal, but only with someone else.

Like a lot of jealousy, justice jealousy can be a signal pointing to many different things,[12] but here I'm just talking about the experience itself. When it turns out that something you needed was, in fact, available—just not to you!—it can be extremely painful. It can also feel like betrayal when your partner has been presenting what you asked for as something they "just couldn't do," and you have done the work to accept things as they are—only to find out that they ... aren't. This betrayal is potent because the harm happens in the gap between what you were told was impossible and what turns out to be selectively possible. This scenario can also generate self-blaming thoughts like "What's wrong with me? Why aren't I good enough?"

It's also worth noting that, depending on the importance of the thing you weren't getting, you may have been self-abandoning[13] when you believed your partner was incapable of meeting your need, and you decided to stay anyway.

PRIVATE DISCLOSURES. In nonmonogamy, where communication

webs are wide, opportunities to disclose private information (intentionally or not) abound, and the stakes can be high. This kind of betrayal can look like members of a polycule, whether partners, metamours, or others more removed, disclosing confidences that you haven't consented to be shared. It may include reading text messages, emails or letters from or to others. When you engage in communication with someone, whether it's text messages or pillow talk, you are operating within an envelope of trust that you have created with that person, and for them to share those communications outside that envelope breaks that trust. The longer these private disclosures go on without you knowing, the worse the betrayal can be.

This kind of thing is very normalized, at least in mononormativity. (Think of Beyoncé singing, "How did it come down to this, scrolling through your call list?") In many circles, people expect to have access to a partner's phone, passwords, emails, text messages—the whole thing. But normal doesn't mean healthy. Reading someone else's private communications can be a sign of coercive control.[14] And even if your partner willingly allows it, it's a violation of the other people who were communicating with them. In nonmonogamous relationships, it's especially concerning, since many communications can be expected to be intimate.

Even if no malice is present, these breaches destabilize the relational safety that nonmonogamy relies on, because autonomy depends on information boundaries being honoured.

"YOU WOULDN'T STAND UP FOR ME." These betrayals happen inside an acknowledged relationship, but they fracture loyalty and shared meaning. They occur when you rely on friends, partners or family to have your back, and they don't. In nonmonogamy, the most obvious of these situations is when a partner allows another partner to veto you, or caves to an ultimatum to end your relationship. Whether or not there was a pre-existing veto in place (that you knew about), this is usually experienced as a profound betrayal. Not only is someone who caves to a veto or ultimatum not standing up for you or the relationship you've built, they are delegitimizing the relationship itself.

More subtle examples of this kind of betrayal might include things like insisting on staying in the closet and keeping your relationship a secret, even if they have the kinds of privilege that would make it relatively safe for them to be out. It could include minimizing your relationship to family and friends (or even another partner) on the grounds that they wouldn't really understand nonmonogamy. If you hold marginalized identities, it could include supporting politicians or policies that harm you. It can feel even worse if they do it because they think they'll receive some other benefit that they care about more than protecting you.

Betrayals About the Relationship

These betrayals do more than break trust; they destabilize the premise of the relationship itself.

POLY UNDER DURESS. Poly under duress (often called "PUD" online) begins when you have been in a monogamous relationship, and your partner tells you that they want to be nonmonogamous, and they essentially give you the choice of agreeing to open up the relationship or losing it entirely.

Now, most "relationship opening up" stories start this way, and they can be hard, but there's nothing inherently wrong with them. If someone realizes that they are nonmonogamous and can no longer be in a monogamous relationship, but they want to stay with their partner, it is (I believe) legitimate for them to give their partner the choice to either open up the relationship or move on, so that each of them can find relationships that they want. Anyone has the right to end a relationship for any reason, and a person has the right to end a monogamous relationship so that they can seek a nonmonogamous one. And if they first want to offer their partner a chance to stay in a previously monogamous relationship by becoming nonmonogamous, that is valid.

However, let's not downplay the pain that this can cause the partner who might not want to open a relationship and who might find themselves ambushed by this request, which can feel like a demand if it puts the relationship at risk. A monogamous partner can experience this conversation itself—the initiation of nonmonogamy—as a betrayal, because the newly nonmonogamous partner is essentially saying they can no longer follow the rules of the relationship that they agreed to at its beginning.

It is to be expected that the person who isn't initiating nonmonogamy might feel betrayed by this request, experience a loss of trust, and need some work to rebuild that trust, even if they agree to practise nonmonogamy. This is particularly true if nonmonogamy was initiated in a way that was not exactly honest; for example, if one partner started another relationship before discussing an agreement to open up—that is, if they're trying to go from cheating to honest, consensual nonmonogamy.

When this situation becomes PUD—a situation of coerced "agreement"—the relationship itself can start to feel like a series of betrayals. When you don't really want to open up, but you agree to it because you're afraid of losing the relationship, you essentially go into nonmonogamy unwillingly. In this case, each new relationship, and perhaps each stage of a new relationship, is going to feel like another betrayal.

I would argue that in this case, the betrayal is often misattributed: You are betraying *yourself* if you accept a PUD situation. That is, you are breaking trust with yourself by acting against your own needs and values. If you accept a relationship with terms that you don't really want and that you know will make you unhappy, then each of the ongoing betrayals that will accumulate as you progress with nonmonogamy actually originate from that self-betrayal.

There is a flip side to this situation, too, which is that if you agree to PUD, you may also be being dishonest with your partner. You might agree to nonmonogamy but not *really* agree to it, and then quietly resist it going forward. Perhaps you don't read the books, join the communities, or do the work on yourself and on your jealousy that you need to do to actually make things work. Maybe you make a ton of rules so you can feel like you're still in a monogamous relationship. And then later on, you say, "Well, I never really wanted to do this in the first place." Now your partner might feel betrayed because you have been dishonest. You agreed to a new circumstance, but you didn't really agree to it (and maybe you blame them, for good measure). The further you go down this path without setting the boundaries that you need to set for yourself, the more hurt you're going to be, and the more shocked your partner is likely to feel if or when you ever do tell them the truth.

Both parties are likely to experience a PUD situation as a betrayal (or a series of betrayals) about the relationship because the partners no longer share the same relational contract, even when everyone is acting with honesty and good intentions.

MISALIGNED EXPECTATIONS. These are implicit expectations that have not been overtly spoken out loud and negotiated. An example of misaligned expectations might be if you assume you will be informed before your partner starts an important new relationship, or at least you'll be kept up to speed as things develop. This expectation might come from very, very valid roots. You may have life entwinements with a partner, and you may have reasonable expectations that your partner will consult with you, talk to you or inform you before they take any steps that might dramatically affect your relationship. But if you've never talked about it explicitly, your partner may not have the same expectations of you, or of the relationship. Or they may not realize just how much their new relationship is going to impact things for you.

Another example might be that you have an agreement to inform each other before you have sex with a new partner, but you haven't discussed what sex actually means. One of you may believe that sex refers to only penis-in-vagina intercourse, and the other person may believe that sex refers to any genital contact (or maybe even sexting!). This kind of misunderstanding is more common than you might think. (Not to mention that defining sex as only penis-in-vagina erases the sexual experience of many queer and trans people, along with a huge part of what counts as sex for many cishet people!)

Again, though, there's another side to this issue. It's also a problem if someone argues that every single thing in a relationship needs to be negotiated for you to be able to have any expectations at all. Essentially, they might say that you are not allowed to expect any kind of baseline if you don't specifically ask for it, which means that you must be able to predict all the ways that your partner might hurt or betray you. If they do something unexpected, you aren't allowed to be upset about it, because you never said that specific thing would be a problem. On my blog a few years back,[15] I called this phenomenon "bees in the closet": "But you never said you didn't want me to start keeping a hive of bees in the bedroom! If you didn't like bees, it was your job to set a boundary about them!" I want to be clear that this is gaslighting, it is potentially abusive, and even as nonmonogamous communities still struggle to define what baselines are appropriate (and thus what kind of advice, validation and support you will receive), it is reasonable to have a baseline expectation of good treatment, honesty, integrity and kindness.[16]

BETRAYAL OF VALUES. These betrayals cut deeper because they don't just violate agreements: They rewrite the worldview you believed you shared. This betrayal occurs when you believe that you and another person (or you and a group) are operating within a shared value system, and then the other person or people unexpectedly act outside it. The shock of this experience can compound when they either don't acknowledge that they're acting outside the value system, or they act as though you were never in that value system together at all. The worst case happens when they reach for normative values to dismiss and invalidate the values you'd previously believed you shared.

As an example, say you are in a queerplatonic relationship—that's a committed, intimate partnership, often a life partnership, that doesn't involve sex or romance. You believe that you are developing a secure partnership with someone, and then they enter a romantic, sexual, possibly escalator relationship. And that's fine, as far as it goes! Queerplatonic relationships can exist alongside more normative ones. But what happens if your queerplatonic partner suddenly stops honouring their commitment to your relationship because they are privileging the normative relationship above your non-normative one? To put it bluntly, the other relationship is more "real" to them (and everyone else) because it fits the societally prescribed mold. This kind of thing can also happen, for example, if you are a relationship anarchist and are focused on developing bonded, committed intimate friendships that are as important to you as your romantic and sexual partnerships, and you think you're doing this with people who share your values. And maybe that works, until one of them gets into a normative partnership and "demotes" you since you are "just" a friend.

This treatment in itself is a betrayal, but it becomes so much worse if they react to you trying to raise the issue with an attitude of, "Well, what did you expect?" Taking this position erases the value of your relationship, delegitimizing it in light of social norms that validate their (probably new) perspective that their new relationship is more important than the one they were building with you.

Or let's say you believe you are in a nonhierarchical polycule. You have a partner who's in a nesting partnership, probably some kind of escalator relationship and maybe one that's older than yours, but who has told you that your relationship is just as real. But they continue to privilege the more normative relationship in ways that are more rooted in assumption and privilege than they are in adequately nurturing the full spectrum of their relationships. And again, if they delegitimize your concerns, possibly delegitimizing and erasing your relationship, it can come with a deep betrayal of values. Perhaps they also use "Well, what did you expect?" to try to make you feel like you're the problem, because it's so easy to fall back on what "everyone" (i.e., the mononormative mainstream) agrees on. You didn't think we really meant all that alternative anarchy stuff, did you? Surely you knew we were just playing around? This kind of invalidation can be very hard, if not impossible, to recover from within the relationship, and it can damage your relating in other relationships over the longer term.[17]

SITUATIONSHIPS AND SCHRÖDINGER'S RELATIONSHIPS. I'm combining these two scenarios here because both hinge on a refusal to name the relationship, or the lack thereof. In both, the betrayal is epistemic: You trusted a reality that the other person never fully acknowledged.

Schrödinger's relationships are somewhat common in nonmonogamy. They occur when it's too painful, or just too much of a hassle, to end or de-escalate a relationship—or maybe you just want the benefits of a relationship without the effort and commitment, or maybe you just don't feel like you need to talk about it—so you invest less and less into the relationship until no one actually knows if you have one or not.[18]

A Schrödinger's relationship is in some ways an inversion of a situationship, which started as a mostly monogamous phenomenon that is increasingly showing up among nonmonogamous folks (perhaps in part because of the mainstreaming of nonmonogamy). In a situationship, you act like you're dating, you have sex and engage in other forms of intimacy, but one or both people resist putting any kind of label on the relationship, setting any explicit expectations, or even talking about the relationship and what it is. If one person wants to make things more concrete, the other might say, "Well, I'm not ready to commit" or "I don't really want to settle down." Or perhaps, "Let's not label things" and its twin, "We don't need a label—why can't we just be together?"

Now, casual relationships are totally fine when they are explicit, everyone is fully on board, and no one is sneaking in expectations or trying to gain some kind of unfair advantage. But situationships as I define them here usually involve some deception or manipulation, even if it's unconscious. To keep these kinds of relationships going (and they are relationships, no matter what they're called), the less invested partner tends to keep the more invested one "hooked" through behaviours like breadcrumbing,[19] engaging in all the elements of a normative romantic relationship except for calling it one (thus involving your attachment system and nurturing a flame of hope that you'll someday be escalated to become a "real" partner), running hot and cold depending on how much you're asking of them (thus conditioning you to minimize your needs), and otherwise making it hard to recognize what's going on, keeping you just attached enough that it's hard to let go.

But the real stunner—and betrayal—tends to come at the end. When someone engaging in these kinds of tactics finally gets called on them, the ambiguity around the situationship can make it easy for them to erase the relationship itself—as though all the intimacy, companionship, shared fantasies, even "I love yous" had never happened.

As I mentioned above, I have no issue with mutually defined casual relationships. Some may find it counterintuitive, but I think healthy casual relationships involve a lot more direct communication than situationships. I see two hallmarks of a situationship that tend to make them dishonest: a tendency to shut down honest conversations about what the relationship is, and a pattern of engaging in the relationship in a different way than it has been explicitly defined.

I think that many people who engage in situationships have a tendency to treat them as though they are relationships. They go to them for sex, support, love, understanding—all of the things that many of us seek from our intimate relationships. People who lean toward *creating* situationships (as opposed to those who *accept* them while wanting something more) often don't want the responsibilities or commitments that tend to come along with these benefits. They don't want to actually have to care for the other person (even if they may care about them, or claim to). They don't want to be needed, to build emotional safety, or to have reciprocity. Because most healthy people would not agree to such an unequal arrangement, people who want situationships often maintain them by acting as though they are in relationships, while never being willing to say that they are.

It's fine to say, "Well, the other person consented to this," but the trick is that this kind of behaviour has a tendency to fool people into thinking that the connection involves real intimacy, something meaningful. And situationships can go on for a very long time—months or even years. Of course, staying in a situationship when you know you need something more is also self-abandonment.

And so, I think that people who are drawn to architecting these kinds of structures are also often (albeit usually unconsciously) looking for people with a specific kind of wounding that makes them prone to self-abandoning.

At the end of a situationship, because no agreements have been made and one person has never explicitly committed to a "partnership" or to reciprocal care (while showing it just often enough to keep the other person hanging on), it's possible for that person to turn around and say, "We were never in a relationship." And even to add the zinger, "You always knew what was going on." So in addition to the pain of losing the relationship, and perhaps the shame of having believed that they were in one, the other person can also experience a profound sense of broken trust. When someone engages in intimacy with us, our bodies tend to respond to that in a trusting way, regardless of what words have been said.

When someone engages in intimacy with us, our bodies tend to respond to that in a trusting way, regardless of what words have been said.

Situationships happen in monogamy all the time, of course. But where nonmonogamy really salts the wound is when the rest of the polycule gets involved. When there are "real" partners in the mix, comparison is easy. Triangulation can also be used as another hook, because if someone confides in you about conflict with a partner or even plans to break up with them, it can feed fantasies of getting "promoted" to partner once someone else is out of the picture.

And here's the additional layer that makes this a distinctly nonmonogamous betrayal: When someone maintains a situationship while also maintaining established partners, the ambiguity doesn't just distort your relationship with them; it distorts your place in the larger relational ecosystem. When the situationship ends, you may lose not only the relationship you thought you had, but also access to community, to belonging, to the sense of being included in the web of care the polycule seemed to offer. Of course, this wider loss happens in ordinary nonmonogamous breakups, too, but a situationship creates the added uncertainty of whether you ever really belonged at all.

As with other kinds of betrayals about relationships, what is betrayed here is not just intimacy, but legibility. You thought you knew the story you were in, and suddenly you don't. That vertigo, the sudden collapse of meaning, is the real injury of situationships in nonmonogamy. They don't just end relationships; they erase them. And that erasure can hollow out your ability to trust your perception of future relationships, because you learned the hard way that intimacy alone does not guarantee reality.

But how do Schrödinger's relationships fit into all this? When it's nonconsensual (some people do agree to them, or at least don't mind them) a Schrödinger's relationship can create its own particular kind of betrayal because it isn't just that someone won't commit—it's that they won't release you, either. Like in a situationship, the relationship exists just enough to keep you tethered, but not enough to give you clarity, reciprocity or safety. This refusal to either show up or step out breaks trust because it removes your ability to orient yourself in the relationship. It's hard to make informed choices when you don't know whether you're in a relationship, ending one, or being quietly phased out. Schrödinger's relationships can betray not only intimacy but direction, keeping you suspended in a place where you can neither fully invest nor fully walk away. Situationships betray you by pretending less is happening than actually is. Schrödinger's relationships betray you by pretending more is happening than actually is.

HEDGING. We're getting close to the end of my taxonomy, and hedging is a particularly severe kind of betrayal. Hedging in nonmonogamy occurs when someone keeps multiple partners around to make sure that they always have someone "waiting in the wings" in case a relationship goes badly. Hedging behaviour also creates a disincentive to invest deeply in a relationship that's having trouble, because if one relationship is in conflict, you can simply go to other partners to make you feel like you're a good person and the other person is in the wrong. This can create a sense of competition between partners, because everybody is competing to be the Good Partner.[20]

This behaviour is a frequent component of abuse in nonmonogamy. But it's also betrayal if you have been in a hedging situation and you didn't know it. That is, if you believed you were both trying to build a healthy, nonmonogamous polycule, and your partner was in it for the long term—but to them, you were always disposable. You trusted that you were in a consensually nonmonogamous situation, where the intention was to build multiple healthy relationships at once, only to find out that you were being played off against another partner.

Hedging can also lead to another particularly damaging situation known as "trading up." This is a tricky conversation to have, because plenty of "trading up" situations in nonmonogamy don't involve manipulation, triangulation or other kinds of sketchy behaviour. It's common for a new partner to raise the bar for what you want in a relationship, or to teach you new things about yourself that mean some of your old relationships may not quite fit anymore. No one has to stay in a relationship that isn't working for them, and it's important to know when to call it before you get too far into a death spiral. But I think it's also important to acknowledge just how painful and damaging such a situation can be for the partner who feels like they've been swapped out. It's basically the nightmare scenario in nonmonogamy—the realization of all the "what if they find someone they like better than me?" fears. Such an experience can make it very hard for the person on the receiving end to have trust in another nonmonogamous relationship.

And sometimes, it turns out to be even worse. Some people simply have a pattern of periodically replacing a boring, stable, longer-term partner with a newer, shiner partner, characterizing every bout of NRE[21] as a magical, game-changing, totally unpredictable bolt from the blue. They may cycle partners directly by breaking up with older partners, but people often do it indirectly by simply disinvesting from and neglecting other relationships, perhaps maintaining one or even several Schrödinger's relationships—thus adding an extra layer of dishonesty and gaslighting to the broken trust.

> Situationships betray you by pretending less is happening than actually is. Schrödinger's relationships betray you by pretending more is happening than actually is.

SECRETLY MONOGAMOUS. This example comes at the end of my list because I believe it is an extreme form of betrayal about the relationship—the entire premise was false, or only conditionally true. It combines several of the other kinds of betrayals: It's a very specific kind of betrayal of values, usually mixed in with some straight-up lies, and maybe some elements of a situationship. In this situation, you believe that you are investing in a real, consensually nonmonogamous relationship with another person who is also nonmonogamous, but you find out somewhere along the line that actually, nope, they are really monogamous, and they knew that all along! Maybe they were dating you because they hoped that they could convince you to be monogamous with them. Or maybe they were doing it because they thought, since you're nonmonogamous, you don't take your relationships that seriously, and so they could treat you as disposable until they found their "real" (monogamous) partner. Or maybe they were, in fact, just dating around until they found their "One," and now that they have finally met that person, they're going to dump all their other partners.

Monogamous dating culture treats multiple early-stage connections as a temporary state on the way to exclusivity; nonmonogamous folks date multiple people because they are open to building multiple relationships, not because they're "shopping" for the one they'll eventually keep. However, the betrayal here isn't just a mismatch of norms: It's the deliberate concealment of an intention that runs counter to the one they claimed to share with you. Someone may call themselves nonmonogamous, or act as though they're open to multiple relationships, because doing so gives them access to connection, intimacy and your emotional bandwidth, while quietly knowing they're eventually planning on an exclusive relationship ... with someone else. When you think you're in a nonmonogamous relationship and you find out you were actually a placeholder on the way to a "real" partner, it can be devastatingly confusing and hurtful. If this is what you're doing, it's dishonest to call it nonmonogamy.

Here, you trusted someone's presentation of themselves as nonmonogamous, and the result was that you didn't know the kind of relationship that you were in the whole time. You invested, maybe deeply. And because of mononormativity, it's again possible to add gaslighting and erasure to this experience, because your partner may act utterly bewildered as to why you would be so upset. After all, they're just doing what's "normal"! You were the one breaking the rules—what did you expect?

Some betrayals happen inside a relationship that is otherwise shared and solid. Others reveal that you were never standing on common ground at all.

* * *

Some of these types of betrayal, as I've defined them, are inherently deceitful and never OK. But for the most part, I'm not really trying to create a moral hierarchy or label anyone as the bad guy. I'm trying to map the terrain of how trust breaks in nonmonogamy, because the kind of rupture you're facing matters. Some betrayals happen inside a relationship that is otherwise shared and solid. Others reveal that you were never standing on common ground at all. The work of repair and the limits of what can be repaired depend on the kind you're dealing with.

Healing from Betrayal

Healing and repairing after betrayal happens along two tracks: the work you do together with the other person (if the relationship survives), and the work you do alone (regardless of whether or not it does). Betrayal rearranges your inner world either way. The question is whether the other person stays in that world as it's being rebuilt. In this section, we'll first explore how healing can happen in the context of repairing the relationship. To start, let's revisit what actually happens—internally—when trust is broken.

When we engage with others, we create mental models of them that we use to predict how they will act. When we first meet someone, our model of them is largely based on our previous experiences of the world, and maybe on people who share some of their characteristics. This modelling process, by the way, is where the idea of "implicit bias" comes from (a term that is usually, but not always, applied to race and ethnicity), but it can apply to just about any kind of input, from the shade of someone's lipstick to the timbre of their voice to the brand of shoes they're wearing—anything

This sort of thing usually ends up poisoning the relationship (with the other and with the self) over the longer term.

that has a strong association for us. We take whatever few informational inputs we have about that person, relate them to our experiences from the past, and create a model of who this person is. As we get to know them better, we (ideally) continually adjust our model to become more accurate to who they are, which requires us to be open to new information about them.

A person's modelling process can be deeply affected by experiences like trauma and past betrayals, so they may be slower to update their models, or they may not be able to update some parts of their model at all. But in general, I'm talking about folks who have a reasonably accurate, flexible and resilient modelling process—at least as much as our flawed human brains allow.

Trust is a component of these mental models. If we want to build a connection with a new person, we have to extend a small amount of baseline trust to them. How much trust we extend at the beginning has to do with our personality and our past experiences. And over time, if the other person acts in a trustworthy way, and our model is flexible, they will build more trust with us—we will begin to see them as a trustworthy person.

When someone betrays you, they introduce uncertainty into that model: Now they are no longer a (fully) trustworthy person. The model that you'd created of them as someone who is trustworthy now has to be adjusted. How much it has to be adjusted depends on the depth of the betrayal, the degree of accountability they take for it, how much they're willing to make amends going forward, your past experiences, and how quickly you're willing or able to update your model based on new information.

For some people, a single betrayal means a person is no longer trustworthy, and therefore is no longer a safe person to be in relationship with. Others will withdraw trust for a time, but are willing to rebuild it. Others will self-abandon, absorb the hurt and let things slide in the interest of protecting the relationship, even though they need accountability and repair. However, this sort of thing usually ends up poisoning the relationship (with the other and with the self) over the longer term.

Self-Repair

We are relational beings. After a betrayal or any other kind of interpersonal rupture, I think the initial instinct for most people is to focus on how to repair the relationship. But first, I want to pause a moment and talk about how we can take care of ourselves after a betrayal, regardless of what the other person does.

> **Healing means slowly testing relationships again—not with unguarded trust, but with attuned trust.**

Being betrayed pulls the ground out from under you. Your body doesn't just lose trust in the other person; it often loses trust in your own perception, especially if you've also self-abandoned. Losing someone hurts, but losing yourself to keep them hurts more. Part of healing is reclaiming your right to expect care, reciprocity and honesty. You do not have to earn those things.

Healing also means slowly giving yourself back the authority to interpret and centre your own experience. Here are some questions that might help—you can try journaling on them, or just reflecting, and see what comes up.

- What did you feel in the moment the trust broke (or you found out about it), and what does that tell you about your needs?

- Where did you ignore your own signals because you didn't want the relationship to change?

- What boundaries did you soften, override or abandon to hold onto the connection?

- What would it look like to honour yourself now, even if the relationship ends?

Worrying that you have a "broken picker" is also a common problem. After a profound betrayal (or several), it's easy to start feeling like you can't trust yourself to choose good partners. This feeling isn't a sign that you're doomed to repeat the pattern, but it is a sign that your nervous system is recalibrating. Betrayal can shift attachment systems, making you either more anxious ("I need a lot of reassurance and consistency now") or more avoidant ("I don't want to risk depending on anyone again"). Neither response is pathological, and both can be adaptive in the short term. Healing means slowly testing relationships again—not with unguarded trust, but with attuned trust. You can learn to notice red flags sooner, name your needs earlier, and walk away from ambiguity before it corrodes you. Just like trust within relationship, this is how self-trust grows back: not all at once, but choice by choice.

I think it is within this process of self-repair that you can come to a decision about how to take care of yourself in this connection: Will you stay and engage in repairing the relationship, or has trust been broken too deeply, such that you need to move on? Neither outcome is a failure. Your task is just to tell yourself the truth about what happened and what you need now.

There's another missing piece here, and it's one that I am still exploring for myself: what to do when the other person doesn't take any accountability at all. It's one thing to hear them apologize but decide you can't continue in relationship with them; it's something entirely different when they won't acknowledge any harm. I think the self-repair process can go a long way to help you heal, but in my experience, it still feels like something is missing. I can say that I have found (sometimes very unexpectedly) significant healing by helping, or even watching, someone else engage in the kind of accountability I needed from someone who betrayed me. I think this effect might relate to something that attachment theory scholar, coach and educator Heidi Priebe has said about how to get closure when a relationship ends badly.[22]

Priebe says that we experience a lack of closure when a relationship ends in the middle of a conflict cycle, during a rupture, without having a chance to progress to repair (even if repair results in the end of the relationship).

She points out that every relationship actually contains two relationships: your relationship with the other person, and your relationship with the version of yourself who exists in relation to the other person. That inner relationship continues long after the other person disappears from your life. You can complete the broken cycle by doing repair with the inner version of yourself: integrating shame, understanding what broke, and defining how you want to show up differently. And because patterns recur, you will continue, for the rest of your life, to meet new people who evoke similar responses from you—and you, too, will have the chance to make different choices. I wonder if my experience of finding healing from another person's

The work of self-repair is not self-punishment.

unrelated accountability may be because it gave the parts of myself that were hurt by betrayal a way to imagine, and thus a chance to internally rehearse, the repair process that I'd needed.

Finally, remember that you are not obligated to forgive, and you are not obligated to stay in connection. You do not have to seek any kind of closure or accept an apology from someone if it will put you back in harm's way. Maybe that's because they haven't really shown you evidence that they've changed, or maybe it's because the damage was so deep that any interaction with them triggers fresh pain. You get to take care of you now.

After a betrayal, you may not know immediately whether you will stay in the relationship or leave it. You may not have a clear sense of how to rebuild your life. But if you can stay, gently and consistently, with your own signals, you can begin to rebuild trust in the one person who will accompany you through every connection you ever have: yourself.

SELF-REPAIR WHEN YOU HAVE BROKEN TRUST

Until now, I have primarily addressed the person who experienced the betrayal. I want to shift gears a bit now and directly address folks who have engaged in some kind of betrayal, who know and agree that they did it, and who want to try to fix their relationships. If the relationship is going to heal, a lot depends on what you do now. You need to be able to step up, take accountability and make active steps toward change. But again, before we talk about making amends with the person you hurt, let's touch on how you can approach that process from a place of wholeness rather than shame.

If you've broken trust, the shame can be brutal. Betrayal wounds the betrayed, but it fractures the betrayer's relationship with themselves, too. You can lose trust in your own judgment, your own integrity, your own sense of who you believed yourself to be.

If that's where you find yourself, the work of self-repair is not self-punishment. It's accountability in the service of becoming someone you can trust again. That work usually starts by telling the truth, not just to the other person, but to yourself. What need were you protecting? What fear were you avoiding? What value did you stop living by? Shame tells us we are our mistakes;

accountability says we did what we did, and we can choose differently.

If the other person accepts your repair, the work continues in the relationship. If they don't, the work continues in you. Integrity is not a reward you earn from others; it's a practice you return to. You can't fix the past, but you can choose how you move forward.

Repairing the Relationship

Now we move from self-repair into the repair of the relationship. In this section, I'm going to keep speaking directly to the person who broke trust, because your choices now will determine whether and how the relationship will continue.

First, let's talk about accepting consequences. I am not talking about consequences in terms of punishment or tit for tat—that leads to toxic cycles and isn't going to heal anyone or anything. But there will likely be consequences in terms of the shape of your bond. If you've betrayed someone, their model of you has probably changed. That can be hard to accept. They may see you as a less trustworthy person than before—but that's because you acted in an untrustworthy way. You've lost their trust, if you haven't lost the relationship entirely.

Especially if you broke the trust of someone you are close to and know well, there's a good chance you know how much damage has been done—for example, if you know any history they have with past betrayals. (Definitely don't use that against them or try to diminish the severity of what you've done.) You must accept that repair often doesn't mean a return to "what was." It means setting aside whatever stories you were telling yourself about how you could get away with it, or it wasn't really that bad, or the other person should just get over it. Instead, repair requires putting yourself in their shoes and acknowledging that your actions had an impact: on them, and now on your relationship with them.

If you're the kind of person who picks up a self-help book called *Nonmonogamy and Betrayal*, you've probably already learned at some point that when someone is upset with you, the first thing you need to do is acknowledge and validate their feelings. But a lot of people stop there, treating these conversations as though their sole purpose is to soothe the person who's upset. If you do this, you may feel like the conversation was a success because your partner was soothed in the moment. You left the conversation feeling good about the connection, so you don't understand why the issue re-emerges days, weeks or months later, or why you keep having the same conversation over and over again. You soothed them—so it was dealt with, right?

What you're missing is that these conversations also involve another piece: The problem itself needs to be addressed in a way that offers meaningful change for the person who was hurt. If you have a pattern of dishonesty that is hurting a partner, then your partner probably wants you to actually address the dishonesty, change it and start being more honest. If there are issues around resources, time, visits and so on, then they need to be addressed. You need to make a meaningful change, or the person who's being hurt by the imbalance or issue will continue to be hurt. (And you're going to continue to have these conversations, and continue to have to soothe your partner.)

Being accountable means accepting the consequences of what you did, and one of those consequences is often that the relationship has shifted. The person you betrayed now trusts you less, and for good reason. Some people resist this kind of change because either they feel too much shame or they just want the relationship back the way it was. But you need to accept that it is going to take time for the other person to trust you again, and that's only if you do better going forward. You may never get the relationship back to the way it was, because you have shifted from someone who has not betrayed them to someone who has. Even if they trust you again, it may never again be the same sort of pure trust that they may have had before. That has to be OK.

It's interesting, too, to reflect on what new inputs you are providing to another person's model during the process of apology and repair. When you give justifications and explanations for your behaviour without reflecting on its impact or making commitments to change it, at some level you are also explaining your own ethical system. You may be communicating that you were not, in fact, on the same page about your shared values. If that's the case, it's reasonable to expect that the other person, if they're responding appropriately, will adjust their boundaries and update their model as a result of the new information about your ethics.

In relationships that continue, repair begins long before forgiveness, or even apology. It starts with an honest inventory of what actually happened, not just externally, but internally. How did trust break? Where did your model of each other shift? What needs to change to make future trust possible? Only after this repair can apology really begin, and it's a different kind of apology than most people are used to.

APOLOGY MEANS ACTION

I remember, when I was a child, saying "I'm sorry" to my mom, and her rejecting my "apology," saying "Sorry means you won't do it again." I had to learn that *sorry* wasn't just a magic word that made whatever bad thing you just did vanish in a little cloud of pink glitter. When dealing with a betrayal in particular, it's important to understand why saying you're sorry isn't actually going to suffice on its own—even if it's a sincere, fulsome apology that shows you understand the damage that was done. Any apology needs to be accompanied by meaningful action: not just a commitment to changed behaviour, but a commitment to the (often slow) process of rebuilding trust by showing someone, over and over, that your behaviour has really changed.

In thinking about repair and apology, I have been heavily influenced by Danya Ruttenberg's book *On Repentance and Repair: Making Amends in an Unapologetic World.*[23] Ruttenberg offers a clear, step-by-step approach to repair based on the Laws of Repentance, part of the Mishneh Torah of Maimonides.[24] This is just one option, of course, and the steps and sequence may not be right for everyone, but it's a helpful way to get you thinking about what the components of meaningful repair might look like to you.[25]

Ruttenberg's steps look like this:

1. NAMING AND OWNING HARM. This isn't the apology—not yet. This is just the acknowledgement: I did that. It hurt someone. This, and confronting the defensiveness and desire to justify your actions, is an important first step.

Ruttenberg points out that there is work to be done even before you get to this step—a "step zero," if you will: listening and understanding the harm. Often, an apology doesn't land because the person never really heard the harm they actually caused—they apologized for something adjacent. Sometimes that's manipulation, but often it's simply lack of skill, empathy or understanding. Before you can name the harm, you must fully listen to and understand it.

2. BEGINNING TRANSFORMATION. To truly make amends, you have to start working to become the kind of person who would not repeat the harm.

3. RESTITUTION AND ACCEPTING CONSEQUENCES. It's not enough just to feel bad and say you're sorry: You have to actually try to repair, to the extent you can, the harm you caused. Of course, it's rarely possible to restore things to the way they were before, but you have to do your best. And what restitution looks like has to be determined in conversation with the person you harmed. That's why this step comes after the previous one—because

if you haven't yet started the inner work of transformation, you're likely to do even more harm when you begin this delicate process of engagement.

4. APOLOGY. Finally, we get to the step that most people want to start with. I think a lot of people assume that step 1 counts as the apology if you include the words "I'm sorry." That is, that taking ownership of the harm is equivalent to apologizing for it. In the framework offered here, though, the apology is something much more. It arises from understanding and action, work that by definition has to take place after the initial owning of the harm. An apology isn't about being forgiven, though this stage (not before!) is when you finally get to ask for forgiveness, if you want to. It's about making the person you harmed feel better. What do they

want to hear? What does a meaningful apology sound like to them? It may not even include saying "I'm sorry." As Ruttenberg points out, an effective apology is done in relationship.

5. MAKING DIFFERENT CHOICES. When faced with the opportunity to commit a similar type of harm, will you make a different choice? Or will you fall back into the old patterns? Actions, not words, complete the process.

Steps 3 through 5 are also where, in relationship, the slow process of rebuilding trust begins. We talked at length about building and rebuilding trust in *The New More Than Two*,[26] but here I will just stress that it can be a long process, as much as you might like for it to be one-and-done. You have to provide enough evidence, over time, that you have changed your ways. In other words, you're trying to retrain the other person's model of you so that it once again predicts your behaviour as trustworthy, and that retraining is achieved through consistency.

What I love about this process is that it offers a pathway for escaping shame—an emotion that can seriously undermine apology and repair, because it puts your ego in the position of defending itself instead of accepting and trying to fix what you broke. These apologies don't neglect feelings, but they are action-oriented and reality-based.

Life After Betrayal

Looking at all these varieties of possible betrayal in nonmonogamy, you might question whether it's worth it at all. (Lots of us don't have that choice, of course, because we experience nonmonogamy as a way of being rather than as an option.) In fact, plenty of people who experience betrayals with a distinctly nonmonogamous flavour do decide to swear off nonmonogamy

> **Betrayal marks us, but it doesn't end our capacity to love or to be loved.**

entirely. That reaction is understandable; when trust collapses within a complex system of relationships, it's natural to want fewer moving parts going forward. But the many ways there are to be hurt can also hold up a mirror to the many gifts of nonmonogamy: the many ways there are to show care and keep trust. In fact, I might well have called this book *Nonmonogamy and Trust*.

But the truth is, no matter what kind of relationships you have, you will, at some or many points in your life, both betray others and be betrayed. Betrayal is part of being human, part of the risk we accept when we let ourselves matter to other people, and part of this fragile but beautiful project called trust. As my friend Shelly wrote,[27]

> There are no good people or bad people here. We only risk becoming something static when

we decide that we've got it all figured out and that our moral code can be absolute. We will all do good things and bad things, and we will all hurt the people we love. Sadly, we will probably hurt them the most in the service of what we believe is right. What makes you good is not perfection in action or strictness to code, but the willingness to question, to change, and to listen to your heart when your life stops matching it.

I might well have called this book *Nonmonogamy and Trust.*

So the question isn't (really) "How do I avoid betrayal?" It's "How do I live after it?" After the ground drops out, what kinds of futures are still possible—both within relationships and outside them? What's on the other side?

Part of my own experience of betrayal has meant grieving the version of myself who trusted so fully before the betrayals happened. I am trying to learn to hold these experiences in balance: honouring myself then for my open-hearted trust, rather than criticizing and judging her for being gullible and naive. Recognizing that she isn't lost to me, not really, but is a continuous part of my trajectory through life—she's still a part of who I am now. Accepting and honouring the person I have become as wiser, more boundaried and more discerning, even where I know the younger me would judge her for being cynical, even cold. Learning that it's possible to be open without being undefended, and to be discerning without being shut down. Accepting that there's no such thing as real safety or perfection in relationships:

I'll still make mistakes, hurt others and be hurt, break trust and have my trust broken, and sometimes put my faith in the wrong people. And remembering that as long as I am still breathing (which will hopefully be a long time yet), I'll always get another chance.

Trust is never a static state. It's something we build, repair and rebuild across a lifetime. Betrayal marks us, but it doesn't end our capacity to love or to be loved. It reshapes us—and sometimes, that reshaping is the beginning of a sturdier, more honest kind of connection, both with others and with ourselves.

Notes

1 Mononormativity is the idea of monogamy as the default, the only "normal" way of having relationships, and the monogamous couple as an organizing unit of society. For more on mononormativity, see Marla Schreiber's *Nonmonogamy and Defying a Paradigm* (Thornapple Press, 2025).

2 *The New More Than Two: A Philosophical Reimagining* will be published in September 2026 by Thornapple Press. This is the paperback format of *More Than Two, Second Edition: Cultivating Nonmonogamous Relationships with Kindness and Integrity*, co-authored with Andrea Zanin, which was published in 2024. We're giving it a new title because it's a misnomer to call it a "second edition": It's a brand-new book loosely based on the framework provided by the 2014 book *More Than Two*. It was confusing, and people kept editing "Second Edition" out of the title. So, new title! The content of the 2024 and 2026 books is the same, so you can pick up either version.

3 Robert Griswold, *Creeds and Quakers: What's Belief Got to Do with It?* (Pendle Hill Publications, 2005).

4 After writing this manuscript, I was reminded of a passage (p. 114) in *The New More Than Two* dealing with *trust* and *faith*, which frames trust in relation to faith in a similar way as I position belief with trust here. I don't necessarily think the ideas in these passages are incompatible, but obviously my understanding and use of the language here is evolving, and I leave it to the reader to choose the framing that works best for them.

5 A relationship that follows an expected set of steps according to mononormative expectations: dating, cohabitation, marriage, maybe kids, death.

6 For more on the security paradox, see Nora Samaran, "For Men Who Desperately Need Autonomy," July 21, 2016, https://norasamaran.com/2016/07/21/for-men-who-desperately-need-autonomy-make-it-dont-take-it/.

7 Another kind of betrayal, institutional betrayal (first described by psychologist Jennifer Freyd), is when someone is harmed by an institution they depend on, such as when legal systems fail to deliver justice to survivors of sexual assault or police violence, or when families fail to protect victims of abuse. That kind of betrayal is beyond the scope of this book, although there are parallels in polycules and communities.

8 With apologies to Andie Nordgren, Meg-John Barker, Mark Michaels and Patricia Johnson, and Amy Gahran.

9 See, for example, chapter 14 of *The New More Than Two*.

10 John Gottman, "John Gottman on Trust and Betrayal," *Greater Good Magazine*, October 29, 2011, https://greatergood.berkeley.edu/article/item/john_gottman_on_trust_and_betrayal.

11 *Polywise: A Deeper Dive into Navigating Open Relationships* (Thornapple Press, 2023), 106–114.

12 See chapter 8 of *The New More Than Two* for a deeper dive.

13 Self-abandonment refers any situation where we chronically fragment ourselves and hide important parts of ourselves, such as our real thoughts, feelings, needs and desires, in order to gain validation, acceptance or approval. For a good discussion, see Heidi Priebe, "Self-Abandonment: What It Is And How To Stop Doing It," October 10, 2022, https://youtu.be/fcRRfH9kowo.

14 See chapter 3 of *The New More Than Two* for more on coercive control.

15 "Bees in the Closet: A Polyamorous Parable," February 16, 2020, https://brighterthansunflowers.com/2020/02/16/bees-in-the-closet-a-polyamorous-parable/.

16 This phenomenon is also discussed at length in chapter 5 of *The New More Than Two*.

17 This extra little twist of the mononormativity knife can certainly come up in other situations described in this section, of course, but I am mentioning it explicitly in those where I think it is most common and painful.

18 See also chapter 21 of *The New More Than Two*.

19 Breadcrumbing is a relational version of intermittent reinforcement, the behavioural pattern where rewards arrive just often enough to keep you invested, but unpredictably enough that you can't tell what will bring them back. That randomness creates a little burst of euphoria when a "reward" lands, which is part of why intermittent reinforcement is so addictive; it's the same mechanism behind compulsive gambling. In relationships, breadcrumbing looks like giving someone small, sporadic doses of attention, intimacy or validation—just enough to keep them from walking away, but never enough to create security or clarity.

20 See *The New More Than Two*, chapters 3 and 8, and Barucha Peller, "Polyamory as a Reserve Army of Care Labor," archived at https://zarinahagnew.gitbooks.io/relationship-explorations/content/second-question.html.

21 New relationship energy, the dopamine- and oxytocin-fuelled heightened state that many people experience in the first couple of months to years of a relationship.

22 "How To Get Closure When A Relationship Ends Badly," May 1, 2023, https://youtu.be/V-MrzWuHUrM.

23 Beacon Press, 2023.

24 This section is adapted from part of an essay I originally published in The Canadian Friend, Winter 2025, 37–40, quaker.ca/cympublications/tcf.

25 Mia Mingus also suggests a similar process in her essay "The Four Parts of Accountability & How To Give A Genuine Apology," published December 18, 2019, at leavingevidence.wordpress.com/2019/12/18/how-to-give-a-good-apology-part-1-the-four-parts-of-accountability.

26 See chapters 5 and 14. Chapter 4 of *Polywise* also offers solid guidance on relationship repair and the tough conversations it can involve.

27 "Guest post: On Zero-Sum, Nonmonogamous 'Family' and Consent," August 21, 2023, at https://brighterthansunflowers.com/2023/08/21/guest-post-on-zero-sum-nonmonogamous-family-and-consent.

About the More Than Two® Essentials Series

More Than Two Essentials is a series of books by Canadian authors on focused topics in nonmonogamy. It is curated by Eve Rickert, co-author of *The New More Than Two*. Learn more at morethantwo.ca.

More from the

More Than Two® Essentials Series

Nonmonogamy and Group Dynamics

Nonmonogamy and Queer Inclusivity

Nonmonogamy and Defying a Paradigm

Nonmonogamy and Happiness

Eve Rickert is a Gen X, queer, solo polyamorous, relationship anarchist, neurodivergent cis woman living on unceded W̱SÁNEĆ and Lekwungen territory on the west coast of the place currently known as Canada. She is the co-author of *The New More Than Two: A Philosophical Reimagining*, the curator of the More Than Two Essentials series and the nonmonogamy resource site morethantwo.ca, the founder and publisher of Thornapple Press, and the founder and mastermind of the science communications firm Talk Science to Me.

PGIL2025USA